G000149545

The Ethics of the
Johannine Epistles

Greg Forster

Rector of Northenden, Manchester

GROVE BOOKS LIMITED
RIDLEY HALL RD CAMBRIDGE CB3 9HU

Contents

Acknowledgments

This study began life as part of a combined book on the Ethics of James' and John's letters. I am grateful to colleagues in the Grove Ethics group for the encouragement to separate the two projects, and for their support as I have written them. In particular Colin Hart set the precedent for these studies, and Dave Leal has made helpful comments on this text, and produced the computer wizardry that enabled the earlier James study to get to the printer. I am also grateful for access to the John Rylands University Library in Manchester. Without that access this book would not have been as comprehensive as it is. But I am also conscious that I have barely touched the surface of what has been written on John's ethics and theology. I hope I have summarized other authors fairly, or at least piloted readers to where they will find the fuller treatment—the short length of a booklet such as this makes it difficult to do justice to all they have written. My own ideas are mostly in the first three chapters, or as conclusions or one line comments (clearly signposted, I hope) elsewhere.

The Cover Illustration is by Peter Ashton

First Impression April 2003
ISSN 1470-854X
ISBN 1 85174 528 9

Introduction

1

Ideally, knowledge of the author, audience, date and circumstances of the Johannine letters would help us understand their ethics.

We know none of these things. The links with John's gospel led to early attribution to the same author, but the gospel is anonymous, and the links may not be straightforward. New Testament ethicists deal with 'Johannine' ethics as a whole, drawing from gospel and letters, while recognizing they may be different stages in development.

Who?

The second and third letters are conventional, though in 2 John a church is addressed as an individual. But 1 John lacks the characteristics of a letter—no greetings, addressees or sender. That spares the dilemma of pseudonymity! If the piece is not by John bar-Zebedee (or a shadowy John the Elder), the 2ⁿᵈ century church made the error. Even the author's claim to eyewitness status may be the voice of the church (1 John 1; compare John 21.24).

The mystery is compounded. The author of 2 and 3 John simply calls himself 'the Elder.' This implies known status. Given his need, however, to put Diotrephes in his place it may be significant that he claims no greater authority, such as we might expect from John bar-Zebedee. Thus, though he speaks by authority his readers can respond according to their conscience. If the author pulls rank, he does so in ways which respect his readers' autonomy. He says a great deal about commands, but in effect appeals to their best judgment, encouraging them to live up to what they know.

Though he speaks by authority his readers can respond according to their conscience

Where?

There is no internal evidence of where the letters come from, but they do point to the circumstances. They suggest churches experiencing, perhaps for the first time, the shock of real schism because of personal differences (3 John) or erroneous belief (1 and 2 John).

3

'Wisdom'?

If 1 John is not a 'letter,' what is it? Judith Lieu notes (1991, p 4) that 'Other categories…have been tried, but most…define the letter's purpose [more] than [reflect] its form in the light of contemporary parallels.' Since she wrote, the idea of Jesus as a wisdom teacher, and parts of the New Testament (notably James) as 'wisdom literature,' has gained favour (Bauckham 2001, Witherington, 1995, ch 7). Perhaps 1 John fits this category. There is an element of encouragement, so the catch-all 'paraenesis' has been tried. But this characterizes many New Testament letters, without demanding the label 'wisdom.'

He was thinking as he believed Jesus might have thought, rather than mouthing the words Jesus said

Bauckham suggests that wisdom teachers reworked sayings of their predecessors. In discussing ethics in the New Testament it is always worth assessing how the author *reused* Jesus' teaching. C H Dodd (1946, pp xxxviii–xlii) analysed the use of the synoptic tradition in 1 John, and found over a dozen parallels. I note that John was confident in reinterpreting some of these sayings—he was thinking as he believed Jesus might have thought, rather than mouthing the words Jesus said. For instance, a coming 'Anti-Christ' is seen in the community's immediate antagonists (1 John 2.18; compare Matt 24.11).

Others of Dodd's parallels are moral aphorisms reworked in a manner typical of the 'wisdom teacher' (for example, 1 John 3.1–3, Matt 5.8–9, and James 1.27). Thus we could see 'wisdom' in 1 John. In contrast to James, however, our writer speaks of 'knowledge,' not 'wisdom from above.' He sees this knowledge in mystical as well as ethical terms. 'You have been anointed by the Holy One, and you all know.' Dodd saw Hellenistic features in this. Since he wrote, the Dead Sea Scrolls have shown such features in Palestinian Judaism too.

He sees this knowledg[e] in mystical as well as ethical terms

Such reworking is characteristic of Johannine Christianity. Dodd and others see difference between the letters and the gospel. This gives our author credibility as an original thinker; he is backtracking from the gospel which portrayed Christ in ways that permitted docetism to grow. Or perhaps we are dealing with one author writing with different purposes. However we answer that riddle, we may usefully compare the ethics of the gospel and letters.

Why?

Our author wrote 'so that you may not sin'—to reassure one section of his churches that their faith was sound, to persuade others not to follow the schismatics, and to denounce schismatic beliefs and morals. This led him so to emphasize love for the brethren that some suggest he has distorted Christ's original teaching of neighbour-love.

The schismatics perhaps saw Jesus as a phantom rather than truly human, or as someone indwelt for a time by a Christ-spirit. For them sin in the material world was irrelevant, or so easily forgiven that it did not affect them, or they were born of God and so did not sin, or what they did was not sin. Each possibility might explain what John says, and matches a later

Sin is real, matters, and is forgiven only at the cost of Christ's real blood

system. In contrast John affirms the reality of Christ's life in the material world, and the importance of moral behaviour within it. Sin is real, matters, and is forgiven only at the cost of Christ's real blood.

In Conclusion

Ironically John's letters seem the most timeless documents in the New Testament, though clearly written for specific situations. They emphasize Christ's earthly reality, and the significance of actual right and wrong, yet their teaching floats almost independent from its precise history. They express most vividly the interdependence of ethics and spirituality, yet contain less detail than most of the New Testament about the minutiae of conduct. Arguably the highest expression of Christian ethics—that God is himself love—is found within them. This vision transcends questions of authorship, genre, and historical situation. Nevertheless, in that actual situation the writer reacts in ways which some see as decidedly unloving!

2   Mystical Ethics

John's ethical teaching appears circular. Love is expressed by keeping Christ's commandment, and he commands love.

But the circle is not closed. John gives examples, refers back to Christ, and assumes a body of Christian teaching which gives love its meaning.

Assurance and Mystical Ethics

John is concerned to give assurance to Christians shaken by schism. Are they truly right with God? John points to their moral practice as grounds for believing they are in the right, but also urges them to keep it up. They can be assured of their status, but cannot rest on their laurels. Moral conduct gives assurance of eternal life. But it is not a motive so much as evidence of what is already true. Love is not a payment for which reward is expected, but a response to love received. They know they genuinely love God because of the practical love they show their fellow Christians, but that love is possible because God's love is working in them already.

Moral conduct is not a motive so much as evidence of what is already true

John's key quality is love, though he also speaks of purity and integrity (truth). These are not simply moral qualities; they have a mystical element too, so that love for fellow Christians whom we see gives substance to the knowledge and love of God whom we have not seen. Our fellowship with them gives meaning to the fellowship we can claim with God if we walk in his moral light. John's moral teaching, therefore, may be thought of as a form of Christian devotion or 'mystical ethics.' 'Ethics' cannot be separated from life in the Spirit; for John there is no such thing as 'autonomous ethics,' though this does not mean Christians abdicate from moral thought. Since God is expressed (though not defined) as love, and love comes from God, the Christian who loves is expressing his God-like qualities and his relationship with God. 'As he is, so are we in this world.' God is pure, so we purify ourselves now, anticipating the time we see him as he is. Perfected love is the aim, and it will quell doubts and fears for that future—in this John refines Matt 5.48 'be perfect...'

This characteristic of John's ethics can lead to confusing ways of speaking. The indicative which describes what we are or shall be contains within it an implied imperative; this is how we should be, and what God makes us, now. This confusion is at its most acute when John speaks about sinlessness. It reflects the tension in the New Testament between the 'already' and the 'not yet' of Christian experience; for Paul too we are already 'dead to sin,' yet have to be told 'not to let sin reign in your mortal bodies' (Rom 6.11–12).

Love for Fellow Christians

Love is exemplified in practical conduct towards fellow Christians; good wishes are not enough (1 John 3.15–18). Again John reflects teaching in Matthew (5.21ff), but here seems to restrict it. Love is specifically for fellow Christians, while Matthew speaks of loving one's *enemy*. The parallel is closer with John's gospel, where the new commandment is to 'love *one another* as I have loved you,' (John 15) in a world which hates Christ and so his people. The outsider gets no mention, except as a source of contamination.

Love is exemplified in practical conduct towards fellow Christians

Is Johannine ethics merely in-group cohesion in the face of hostility, or is this introversion a necessary response to such hostility, and a means of creating a community which is a moral training-ground and an example and challenge to the loveless world? Or does John focus in these letters on love within the fellowship because his teaching on assurance depends upon it—no experience is truly Christian if it does not lead to practical love for one's fellow Christians? Whatever the truth, it is unfair to single out John for criticism. Paul speaks about doing good to all, *especially the household of faith* (Gal 6.10), Peter speaks of the importance of love for the fellowship, and James applies a similar test for faith that is real (James 2.14ff). John's turn of phrase may be his own, but his teaching is mainstream.

John's turn of phrase may be his own, but his teaching is mainstream

The Pattern of Good and the Source of Evil

For John the Christian's moral standing is threatened by the world and the evil one (and the flesh, although Christ 'came in the flesh' too). He is called to walk in the light, and so to avoid the darkness around. But John scarcely fills out the commandment of love. Perhaps he believed that the Spirit that anointed the church would guide it into moral truth (compare 1 John 2.20). I suspect as well that he could draw on a body of truth which his churches knew 'from their beginning,' concerning Jesus and his teaching. They ought to 'walk as he walked' (2.6). The Jewish term for moral teaching is *halakhah*— 'the walk,' while the church in Acts is called 'the Way.' Even the recurrent theme of Christ's 'commandments' has a Jewish background, in which we are not talking about 'battlefield orders' but a rule of life which is at its best a source of joy, a link with one's community, past and present, and a sign of a right relationship with God whose *gifts* the commandments are. We may not know in detail what John expected of his churches, but that is not the same as saying that *they* did not know. For him love sums this up.

To walk in the light of Christ involves recognizing one's own sinfulness

To walk in the light of Christ involves recognizing one's own sinfulness, and accepting forgiveness based on Christ's death. To deny this, as John's opponents apparently did, is to lack the integrity which accepts God's verdict on the world. That world may be in the grip of the evil one, but he is not an agent who overrides people's moral responsibility, though he is the source of sin. Cain (1 John 3.12ff) may have been of the evil one, but his murderous action had grown from persistent wrong action and hatred—a character developed over the years. John 'demythologizes' the 'Sin-demon crouching at the door' of Genesis 4, as he demythologizes 'Anti-Christ' at 1 John 2.18. We cannot find excuses in some supernatural force. John's understanding of human moral nature is therefore naturalistic, though conversely he turns to God to override the too sensitive human conscience (1 John 3.18). He knows everything, not in the sense of catching us out, but as someone who understands and accepts.

God knows everything, not in the sense of catching us out, but as someone who understands and accepts

Twice John seems to offer a definition of wrong. 'In fact that sin is The Lawlessness,' (1 John 3.4) and 'Every unrighteousness is sin' (5.17). In both cases we are dealing with a point made in a context, as my translations emphasize. John's opponents look for some cataclysmic end-of-time 'Lawlessness' or denounce the pagan world as 'without our Torah.' Their own behaviour fits that bill (3.4)! No-one could excuse minor peccadilloes—it all matters, but may be forgiven (5.17).

Controversies

In John's letters we see ideas which have been controversial in Christian moral teaching. Two are mainstream; the third is liminal. 1 John 5.16ff speaks of 'sin which is mortal' and talks of how one Christian may pray for the reconciliation of another. In ch 3.4–9 he suggests that those born of God cannot sin. These issues surface less starkly elsewhere in the New Testament.

Mortal Sin

Whatever John meant by 'a sin which is mortal,' it is not what is understood by 'mortal sin' in Catholic moral theology. That is a class of sin which needs confession and priestly intervention. Here John suggests something for which prayer is not effective. This is itself a puzzle, since he said earlier that the blood of Christ cleanses from *all* sin. He may be referring to deliberate sins which the Old Testament taught were not expiable through the sacrificial system (see Leviticus 4), or to those which led to a physical death penalty. In Hebrews the writer speaks of apostasy as something from which a believer cannot return (Heb 10.26–29). More likely in our context is the similar suggestion that schism—separation from Christ's church—is unforgivable, since one cuts oneself off from the source of forgiveness. This would be a legitimate extension of the 'blasphemy against the Holy Spirit' in the gospels (for example Mark 4.28f) where Jesus' power for good is ascribed by his enemies to Evil.

However, John's point is that Christians should pray for each other for release from sin. In the heat of controversy he suggested that schism was beyond redemption.

Intercession and Absolution

Once again, what John describes is not later penitential practice. James encourages intercession for Christians who get into moral trouble, with perhaps a special role for the elders, though confession and prayer is mutual (James 5.15–20). Paul encourages gentle correction (Gal 6.1f) by any 'who have received the Spirit,' which does not imply a special order.

What all speak of is moral counsel and prayer. We find absolution, perhaps, at John 20.23. If so, does the letter tone down that verse in the light of John's opponents' cavalier attitude to sin? Is he saying, 'in spite of what you have read, don't expect to clean every slate just on your say-so'?

Motives and Moral Energy

If for John the greatest sin is schism, and the key to moral behaviour is love for the brethren, the inspiration which motivates such human love is God's love for us, shown in Christ's real coming and self-sacrifice. 'We love because he first loved us.' Once again, John is putting in his own words a thought common to the New Testament. 'Welcome one another,' says St Paul, 'as God in Christ has welcomed you' (Rom 15.7). But the love of God is not just a moral quality, or even a moral imperative, but almost an entity which is shared with the believer. It seems almost a synonym for the Holy Spirit (1 John 4.11–17). The eternal verity which is love receives a form in the life of the believer, thus his commandments are not burdensome. God supplies the moral energy to observe them, and through his Spirit guides the church as to what it might require in its current situation.

It is tempting to see in this an insight similar to the modern psychological understanding that being loved offers the security from which we in turn can love. While this is true, John is saying something bigger—God's love can support us where human love is deficient. He adds a further psychological dimension, in recognizing the overactive conscience (1 John 3.20). God's love overrides our self-doubts.

The eternal verity which is love receives a form in the life of the believer

Moral behaviour contains an assurance of our relationship with God. For John this is not so much a motive, but evidence vouching for the prior existence of the relationship. John slips between affirmation of his readers' faith, and exhortation to them to abide in God's love in ways which exercise moral responsibility. Though he relates this love to the observation of Christ's commands, the fact that this command is expressed in general terms implies that he is trusting them to apply in detail the principles that they learn from him and have learned from Christ 'at the beginning.'

He offers two primary examples of what this might mean—in the gospel the foot-washing story and in the letter the injunction to share with those in need. He may also have expected the Spirit to inspire *in the community* knowledge of how to respond in specific situations. He refers to walking as Christ walked, and may have had a body of Christian *halakhah* in mind. But he promotes that loving way of life in a far less prescriptive way than that found in Jewish or even other New Testament writers. Formally his ethics are deontological—shaped by duty—since friendship with Christ is shown by obedience to him, yet in practice he leaves much to the believers' conscience.

'Agape-Love'

Love is at the centre of John's thinking about Christian morality, and about God himself. However, he does not say that love is God, but that God is love—that is, his activities are characterized and controlled by love. Thus his justice should be understood as motivated and shaped by love, not anger.

What does John mean by love? He reports Jesus' commands, and instructs his churches to 'love the brethren.' Love for God is to obey the commandment, and the commandment is to love God and the brethren. The washing of the disciples' feet is an example from which the implications of love can be generalized, while Jesus speaks of his own death as demonstrating the greatest love. 1 John's readers are told that this love might mean death—and lest they take refuge in grand gestures are immediately told about sharing the next meal (1 John 3.16ff). Like James or Paul, John expects action (James 1.22, Rom 2.13, Col 3.12–14, 1 John 3.18).

The word love—*agape*—is not John's own but common Christian usage, in preference to the normal Greek words—*philia* or *eros*. Maybe this was influenced by the sound of the Hebrew *'ahabah*. The noun occurs in the Septuagint (LXX), the Greek Old Testament dating from about 250 BC. The verb is older and is not specially 'pure.' LXX Jeremiah used it of prostitution (LSJ 1940, Edwards, 1996 p 85)!

20th/21st Century discussions use *agape* to characterize selfless or spiritual love in contrast with *eros*, but that is not ancient usage. *Eros* in Hellenistic philosophy denoted a pure craving of the soul for the divine. The root meaning of *agapao* was 'welcome or treat with affection.'

The Christian use of the word must be derived from Christian teaching. For John the meaning is set by Christ's example. It includes feelings and mystical devotion, but must be sacrificially practical and is rooted in a historic revelation and redemption (4.9, 10). It is the primary characteristic of God, and only when believers show a Godlike love for each other can they honestly claim to know God (4.7, 8, 20). To love, then, is not just a moral duty for Christian believers; it is an act of devotion, and an experience of being caught up into the presence of God (4.11, 12). This is a bolder understanding than we find elsewhere in the New Testament. Even Paul's prophetic description (1 Cor 13) simply elevates a moral principle that should shape all conduct within the church.

3

Comparison of the Letters with the Gospel

In 'The Ethics of the Gospels' in this series Colin Hart identified five characteristics of John's gospel:

1 'dualism';
2 the Old Testament as a source of prediction about Jesus, not ethics;
3 faith as the 'work' God expects, by which believers anticipate judgment;
4 the imitation of Christ in bearing testimony with the Spirit as a witness;
5 the 'love command' as central, but focused within the disciples.

1 Dualism

The dualism contrasting the believing community with the world seems stronger in the letters than in the gospel. It seems a concession that Christ died for the sins of the whole world (1 John 2.2), for the world is gripped by the evil one (5.19). Indeed, former members of the community are 'antichrists,' so strong is John's sense of 'them' and 'us.' John now focuses on the pure community, not God's kingdom.

Dualism—Background and Definition

This word centres on the polarization of reality into opposed states. It describes various simplistic ways of dividing the world into right and wrong.

The Dead Sea Scrolls community made a distinction between 'the sons of light' and 'of darkness.' They almost treated this division as predetermined, though only after commitment to the community did this become apparent.

Like Judaism in general they distinguished between 'this age' which is lawless and destined to pass away, and 'the coming age' when God sets injustices right (and restores Israel). This dualism is moral and temporal.

Various 'Gnostic' groups in the second century distinguished between the pure world of the soul, the realm of the enlightened and of the supreme God, and the evil world of matter from which right thinking people sought separation (by asceticism or excess). For them the idea of the Word, God's self-expression, becoming flesh was a contradiction in terms. The dualism here is timeless, but centred on spirit or mind, and matter.

Many dualisms had a deterministic view of these divisions, so that to be on the 'good' side was to have rediscovered one's destiny or true nature.

1 John is not entirely dualistic, but comes close to several of these types, so that some writers ask critical questions about John's Christian credentials. He writes for an 'in-group' and his criticisms are reserved for deserters. They seem to have been more dualistic, rejecting Christ's incarnation and the seriousness of wrongdoing. Yet John affirms creation and the value of practical love here and now, even if the world is in the grip of evil.

Dualism is a cast of mind which prefers easy labels to moral evaluation of each case or character. It infiltrates 21st century political thinking and international relations as easily as theology and spiritualities.

2 The Old Testament

The letter-writer scarcely acknowledges the Old Testament, though when he does it *is* as a moral example (1 John 3.12, Cain and Abel). He makes a dualistic point about the brothers, but their actions, not destinies, mark whose side they are on.

3 Faith, Works and Judgment

In 1 John the faith which is crucial has strong doctrinal overtones lacking in the gospel. Eternal life in John 17.3 is *knowing* God and his Christ; in 1 John relationship—with God and fellow believers—remains, but is overlaid by a doctrinal test—to confess the Son is to know the Father (1 John 2.23). The crucial 'work' which God expects is love for the brethren, as a tangible sign of love for God himself. This is not rejection of the gospel's 'faith' but changed emphasis in reaction to schism.

What is significant is the kind of judgment the letters anticipate. Like the gospel they speak of having passed from death to life (1 John 3.14)—a kind of pre-emptive judgment such as found in John 3.18—but alongside the gospel's criterion of belief is love for the brethren. Once again circumstances lead to changed emphasis. But in 1 John the judgment, however it may be prefigured in present behaviour, is a thing for the future. The world is passing away (2.17). Time shall be when we reflect Christ's glory (3.2). When that judgment comes those who love God may have confidence (4.17). This contrast between gospel and epistles seems so strong that Houlden (1973, pp 16–20) argued that the letters try to return innovative theology in the gospel towards a more 'traditional' view of the last judgment. However, the gospel also includes the more 'traditional' expectation (John 5.27f; 6.39f; 12.48). Houlden resolves this by postulating revision within the gospel to correct 'Gnostic' reading of a first edition. Without this hypothesis we may allow that the letter down-plays the pre-emptive concept of judgment which the schismatics appropriated from the gospel.

4 Imitation of Christ and the Work of the Spirit

In the letters, the believers' likeness to Christ is both mystical and moral. They can find reassurance that their rejection by the world was what their Lord also knew (1 John 3.1, compare John 15.18–24). They are also challenged to purify themselves as he is pure (3.3), and may have confidence for the day of judgment when their imitation of him leads them to a perfection of love (4.17). This echoes Matthew 5.48 more than John's gospel, and is a more ethical understanding of the imitation of Christ than the gospel's, despite 20.21.

In the letters, the believers' likeness to Christ is both mystical and moral

In discussing John's gospel, Hart suggests that the Spirit is not a moral force, as in Galatians 5.22f, but a source of life, strength and illumination. The same is true in the letters, unless the 'truth' which the Spirit reveals is moral guidance as well as doctrine, or (as Hart tentatively suggests) ethical integrity. But would John have drawn distinctions here? The good life is friendship with Christ in the Spirit.

We might add that in John's gospel the Spirit is the source of the church's forgiving authority (20.22f). In the letters this ministry is limited to prayer in some circumstances (1 John 5.14–17). Perhaps the schismatic people of the Spirit were too ready with their absolutions.

5 The Love Command

Hart highlighted the 'Love Command.' In the letters this is just as prominent. The writer plays with the catchphrase *a new commandment* (John 13.34, 1 John 2.7f), and weaves his letter around love for the fellowship. It is old, because they heard it when they came to faith (1 John 1.1, 3). It is new, because of the new light in their lives. In the gospel, Christ's love for the disciples inspires love (also 1 John 4.7–12). This will bear witness to the unbelieving world. In the letter, witness recedes and love for the fellowship becomes a touchstone of closeness to God.

Hart suggests that in John's gospel no link is implied between loving God and loving one's *neighbour*. Love is for fellow believers. The letters further emphasize that without love for fellow Christians any love for God is a sham. The polemic circumstances of these letters have, ironically, produced some of the most eirenic affirmations of Christian care in the New Testament! Strictly, the writer did not expect this standard to be applied universally (he draws the line at the schismatics—2 John 10!). This contrasts with 'Love your enemies...' (Matt 5.44) though the later church has often ignored this difference.

'In the Flesh...'

A further common emphasis in the gospel and these letters is the coming of Jesus as Christ *in the flesh*. The reason is doctrinal, not ethical. Both have a high view of Jesus as Son of God and Messiah, but make it clear that he was truly human. He was no phantom or divine spirit inhabiting a human body. But they do not go on to propound a 'world affirming' view of Christian behaviour or involvement with 'the world.' That is for them hostile, rejecting the Messiah and his followers, and to be rejected in turn by them (for example 1 John 4.4–6). Indeed, for the gospel, it is by its reaction to the light of the incarnation that the dark world brings judgement on itself (1.5, 10; 3.19, 20)! The writer(s) might be surprised to see how Christians over the last century take this incarnational theology to justify involvement in politics, the arts, and such like. Yet, in the light of the synoptic accounts of Jesus' lifestyle and teaching, such affirmation of the incarnation surely leads the church (when not a persecuted minority) away from rejecting what is wholesome in God's world.

To Sum Up...

There are different emphases in John's gospel and these letters. Whether one author or more were at work in changed situations is not our primary concern. They are on the same trajectory. Perhaps that led to the dead-end of sectarianism. Along the journey, however, new vistas are revealed on God's love and the reality of his commitment to creation. These have inspired Christian ethics subsequently.

3 John—the Sin of Schism

Nothing in 3 John requires connection with the heresies of 1 and 2 John. The Elder does not accuse Diotrephes of wrong teaching. But in this personal letter we find matters the Elder regarded as ethical, though we might not think of them so.

Diotrephes is criticized for pushing himself forward (a secular virtue! LSJ 1940), for not welcoming the Elder's emissaries and thus breaking fellowship, and for slandering him and driving people from the church who were friendly towards him. Gaius is commended for supporting these emissaries who chose not to accept help from pagans. Emphasis is placed on acting 'according to the truth.'

The emissaries take seriously Christ's injunction to go nowhere among the gentiles (Matt 10.5), or its application, 'keep oneself unspotted by the world' (James 1.27). They work within the assumptions of the mainstream church of the 1st century. Moreover, Diotrephes perhaps flouts the secular norms of his day—to be hospitable to one's 'guest-friends.' This also ignores a Christian obligation which was treated as a Spiritual gift (1 Pet 4.9, Rom 12.13, Heb 13.2). This might prove onerous, and the Elder expresses thanks for Gaius' hospitality. Ironically, in 2 John 10 he advises Christians *not* to welcome unorthodox missioners. Is he guilty of double standards? Presumably he does not regard Diotrephes as heretical, merely discourteous and self-promoting, so a different principle applies.

Self-promotion is another vice which the wider church saw as a danger to unity (James 3.14, 16; Rom 12.3 and Heb 13.17). It led Diotrephes into sin. The Elder does treat it as sin, not as a 'personality clash' as we might in some 21st century dispute. It divides the church and is a serious issue. In 1 John we read that the letter's purpose was not just 'that you may not sin,' but also 'that you may have fellowship with us' (1.3). John almost treats these two phrases as synonymous.

Such partnership was a high virtue in the early church, and seems to be a principle which governed other problems: hospitality and brotherly love are virtues; restoration to fellowship is a high ideal (James 5.19; Gal 6.1; 1 John 5.16); there is one Spirit, however many gifts he gives (Eph 4.2–7; 1 Cor 12.12f; Rom 12.4f). Paul subordinates other questions to the obligation to maintain unity of faith and fellowship (Rom 14.19; see also v 15 and 15.5 and James 4.11). Diotrephes' snub is a challenge to the identity and purpose of the church, and though orthodox, his schism is sin, not just a personal affront.

What the New Testament Ethicists Say

4

Ethicists tend to treat these letters as one corpus with the gospel, while recognizing that the authors may be different.

They represent a particular ethos, perhaps at different stages of development. I have singled out comments on the letters where possible and fair to the modern author.

Jack Sanders

The Johannine letters are criticized as liberally as John criticized his opponents. Jack Sanders (1986, pp 91ff) typifies this. The 'wonderful ethics' of the New Testament was eschatological, but John reinterpreted it. The end time has already arrived within the church (he follows Bultmann, blaming futurist eschatology on a redactor). John's 'simple ethics' is intended only for the church (p xiv). John altered the synoptic command to love one's 'neighbour.' In his letters love applies only to one's 'brother.' Bultmann was wrong to pretend that this includes the neighbour since the community was open to all. John changed the synoptics deliberately.

He suggests that this narrowing derived from the church's conflicts not just with Judaism and Hellenistic paganism but also with an early Christian Gnosticism. Thus an unlimited care towards fellow human beings is transformed into a love which evangelizes a hostile world before it cares for the converts. This is ethical 'tunnel vision,' characteristic of John's writings. 'The only good one can do for one's fellow man is to witness, so that he may believe and believing have life' (1986, p 97).

This ethics boils down to the welfare of fellow Christians. No-one is too high or too low for this duty—he correlates Christ's footwashing with 1 John 3.16f and translates v 17 (*echei ton bion*) as 'whoever draws breath,' that is, all—however poor they are. The Christian task is living in this hostile world as the eschatological community, for which heavenly standards already apply. The tension elsewhere in the New Testament of 'already but not yet' is resolved. For the in-group the 'already' is here.

Sanders does not like this picture. It is 'precisely the ethics of the new fundamentalism.' This sheds as much light on Sanders as on John. He wrote in the early 1970s, in West Coast America at the height of the 'Jesus Movement.' In the 'proliferation of such fundamentalist groups' he saw evidence of 'the weakness and moral bankruptcy of the Johannine ethics.' He scathingly contrasts John's 'Are you saved, brother?' with the Good Samaritan, or Paul's 'love is the fulfilling of the law.'

Gerd Theissen

Writers with a sociological perspective take a different approach. Gerd Theissen sees a trajectory in the New Testament towards this introversion, and cites Paul's 'do good unto all, *especially the household of faith*' as a stage along that road (1993, p 265f). This is a means of integrating people, some very much underdogs, and giving them self worth when few of them had status in society.

Leslie Houlden

Leslie Houlden is not as scathing as Sanders, but he too has a low opinion of John's ethics. It 'accords a minimal role to autonomous ethics' while 'the world, as a scene of moral problems, is absent' (1992, p 35). The believer has no moral duties to the world. The fellow Christian, not the 'neighbour,' is to be loved. For John this could hardly be otherwise, for only within the church did moral significance lie; the world outside was as good as passed away.

Houlden comments that few Christians now take John so literally as to exclude the world outside the church from their moral concerns. But in understanding John we cannot assume that his readers have read the synoptic gospels and espoused the ethical teaching of Jesus as reported in them. We should read him on his own terms. The crowning commandment, to love, is the sole one. That love is sustained by the love of believers for Christ, and *vice versa*, which in turn catches them up into the Father's love for the Son. John's primary concern is not, then, ethical, but devotional.

1 John has, at first sight, a greater ethical interest than the gospel, but 'the appearance deceives.' Love is the only virtue, except perhaps purity; the frequent references to Christ's commandments are never specific; hatred is the sin *par excellence*. Love is the moral expression of 'walking in the light' and other religious states. So there is an intimate connection between belief and conduct.

Houlden speaks of John's dualism. There is division between the circles of light and darkness, and no obligation to love outside the circle of light, since the world is in the antichrist's power and is fading away. But this does not lead John into the extremes of the Gnostics, for Christ 'came in the flesh.'

Loving fellow Christians is an end sufficient to itself, though a hope of transfiguration is a further spur to virtue.

Houlden notes how John's stress on the incarnation is taken as hallowing human society and social action. John did not intend this—the pressures on his churches were different from the industrial society which prompted this—though it is not an inappropriate interpretation.

Wolfgang Schrage

Schrage's criticism of 1 John as ethics is more academic (1988, pp 295ff). He questions 'whether a chapter on the Johannine writings belongs in...the Ethics of the New Testament, or would be better...in [its] Theology...' In the Epistles he recognizes paraenesis (a moral genre), dualism and intra-community love. In gospel and epistles ethical dicta are integrated into the theology differently from other NT writings—being and doing are identified practically.

Schrage begins his account of John's ethics with a discussion of Christology. Through his presence in the flesh we behold Christ's *glory*. John's emphasis lies with glory, not flesh. A Christian's role is to glorify God by 'bearing fruit,' and this is done by 'abiding' in Christ (John 15.8ff). The source of Christian virtue is abiding in Christ. Conversely, the branch that does not bear fruit is cut off. Here, in Johannine language, we see the NT tension between faith, grace and works. Similar language appears in 1 John, where the ethic of love is rooted in and empowered by the love which God has already shown. 'Love cannot be separated from Jesus and made an ethical principle or programme, practiced apart from him' (p 301).

Keeping the commandments is John's key summary of ethics, but these are not the Old Testament Decalogue but Jesus' Word of love, exemplified in Jesus' own self sacrifice. Conformity to Jesus' conduct fills out John's ethics (Schrage too links the footwashing and 1 John 3.15ff). Jesus himself replaces the law of the Old Testament (pp 306, 308). The reference to Cain indicates familiarity with the Old Testament, but its rules have no ethical standing.

Schrage notes John's dualism between the Spirit and the world. The world threatens believers, but John does not indulge in total world denial. His doctrine of creation is too strong for that. Only in gospel (3.16) is there a positive expression of God's love for the world, though his mission of saving it runs through the gospel and 1 John 2.2. This is not a basis for Christians' ethical relationship with the world, only for their witness.

Discussion of dualism leads Schrage to consider sinlessness. Logically we might expect John to say that separation from the world means freedom from committing sin. He does not. That is his opponents' position. Though he sees it as an aim, in reality 'we deceive ourselves' if we claim it now. John's aim in speaking of this is 'paraenetic; to mobilize Christians to do battle against sin' (p 313).

Schrage feels on less sure ground at 1 John 5.16f where John speaks of a sin which cannot be remitted. He points out how John contradicts himself. Earlier he asserted that Christ's blood cleanses from all sin, or that theoretically any sinning demonstrates that the sinner is not born of God. Now he divides sin into different categories and degrees of seriousness. Schrage does not wish to exonerate sin, but does criticize the view that certain sins should not call for intercession or invite forgiveness (p 314).

Finally, the law of brotherly love. This is the only commandment in John's writing, and is described as 'new.' Is it new because it relates to the eschatological new world, or to the new covenant—or has Jesus' love introduced a new dimension, ultimately revealed in his self sacrifice? In the epistles there is a dual reference. The commandment is new, in theological terms, yet old in the sense of Christian tradition, and in 2 John 5 the Elder seems to appeal to the authority of tradition as well as the original revelation. There is also a qualitative newness about this love. Schrage does contrast *agape* with the *philia* of Hellenism, which had connotations of self-fulfilment, eros and self-promotion. Here is a love which is altruistic, modelled on Christ's self-giving.

However, John's use of 'new' is inappropriate. He has reduced the 'radical inclusiveness' of Jesus' Good Samaritan, and love for one's enemies, to an exclusive concern for 'the brother.' 'Do not even the gentiles love those who love them?' Despite references to mission, John is primarily concerned with the in-group. Schrage notes how commentators mitigate this: a loving in-group can be attractive to in-comers; love for enemies is pointless if the church is rent by mutual hostility; the context is bitter persecution. 1 Peter similarly encourages *philadelphia* as the community faces persecution. This may explain, but surely does not justify, 'a particularistic, conventicle ethics' (p 318)!

John's exclusivism is not antagonistic. He does not encourage *hatred* of the persecutor or outsider, as we find in Qumran. Love for the community will commend the faith, and is severely practical. He may speak of loving fellow believers to the point of death, but also talks about their next meal, an immediate concern. In this concern for practicalities John's ethics comes back to its roots, as seen in the writing of James or the practice of Jesus.

Richard B Hays

Richard Hays approaches NT ethics differently. He recognizes that eschatology played a major part in the behaviour of the early Christians, but prefers describing the *moral vision* of NT authors and how that vision was embodied in their churches. This gives him a favourable view of John, since here is a distinct emphasis on how a community shapes up to challenges. In discussing the formation of communities which model Christian ethical standards Hays draws heavily on 1 John. Its vision of love shapes Christian views on marriage, even though that is not mentioned in the letter (1996, p 375ff).

Like our previous examples, Hays notes the lack of specific commands except to love, and the lack of reference to the OT law except as a kind of prophecy. John's ethics is intra-communal, and was used by H R Niebuhr to exemplify the ethical stance in which *Christ* is *against Culture*. Houlden or Sanders see this as a deficiency in John's attitude; Hays claims that they are 'too hasty.' John must be read more deeply. He uses his whole story to shape a community. Perhaps he does emphasize a 'man from heaven' Christology, but he stresses true incarnation, and 'the importance of this fact for ethics is considerable' (p 142).

There is a strong devotional element in John's view of Christian behaviour. Abiding in Christ and following his example determine the community's norms. But in context the command to love does not end in 'sentimental complacency, but the cross.' In economic behaviour this has implications at odds with both ancient and modern commercial convention (1 John 3.16–18). Such attitudes are 'dramatically counter-cultural.' Furthermore, Christ's death was for the whole world, which gives a wider reference to 'love one another' than the community alone. Hays wryly comments that the need to stress love within the community is demonstrated by the historic levels of acrimony within the church, and concludes, 'this may not be the last word to be said about Christian ethics, but it is not a bad place to begin' (p 146).

This appeal for love was made in the context of Christian expulsion from the synagogues, and subsequent internal schisms in the church. The psychological integrity of a shaken community was at stake. The eschatological promise had been refocused (as the first generation died) onto a present experience of the values of the kingdom. If those loving values were now destroyed, what hope was there?

John is notorious for not giving specific content to his ethics. Hays suggests that the specific injunctions found in the synoptics or Paul were replaced, for the Johannine community, by the guidance of the Paraclete, received through prophetic speakers (see 1 John 2.21, 27). Yet even that was being called into question by the presence of rival charismatics (4.1, 5)! So a doctrinal touchstone is introduced.

Hays is reluctant to rely on the redactor to explain futurist eschatology. 'We have only the text before us.' John does not supplant the future hope, but emphasizes the present fullness of life for those who believe. Ethical norms lie in conformity to the person of Jesus. Future rewards or punishments play a minor role in his ethical motivation. However, the conundrum of asserting that believers cannot sin (1 John 3.9) is an indicative, not a hidden imperative, and the tension created by this is resolved in the light of the future hope expressed in the preceding verses (3.2, 3).

John's moral vision is one in which time future is merged into time present while the contrast between moral light and darkness is stark. Rejected from its Jewish cultural roots, the church stresses fellowship, has no hierarchical structure and treats women as equal in discipleship (apparent in the gospel). Sin is rejected, but claims to sinlessness are exposed as deceitful. Righteousness is exhorted though little is said of its details. The distinguishing mark of the community is not sinlessness but a willingness for sin to be brought to the light, confessed and forgiven. The incarnation deconstructs dualism—earthy symbols such as water and blood express Christ's work and nature sacramentally and affirm the goodness of creation even if the world as culture is hostile to God. Thus, Hays concludes, Sanders has missed the point with his 'Are you saved?' caricature of John's ethics (p 157).

Hays draws attention to anti-semitism in the New Testament, especially in John's gospel, though religious quarrels, not racial prejudice, prompted it. We cannot make the excuse that this refers to leaders, not Jews as a whole. Real antagonism arose from closure of Jewish communities to Christian Jews around 85 CE. In John's letters, I note, there is no apparent anti-Judaism, though if Hays is right, this rejection influenced John's *laager* mentality in relation to his heretics (p 407ff, especially p 424ff).

Conclusions

There is an old warning about finding what you started from. These New Testament ethicists risk this, though not always unhelpfully. Sanders' view is coloured by negative experience of Christian cults and his own world-affirmation. Houlden holds moral autonomy highly, so is not impressed by John's vague, devotional deontology. Schrage is not so critical. He recognizes John's social climate, and despite the theological orientation and social introversion of the letters, he recognizes their severely practical applications of brotherly love as true to Christian roots. Hays, more true to the cultural patterns of the New Testament, looks for communal visions and values and sees them in action in John. This kind of ethical study matches the value ethics which have been in vogue since the 1990s.

Sinless Perfectionism?

5

Can Christians sin? Through church history groups have answered 'No.'

Their consequent behaviour was sometimes bizarre if not licentious. Mainstream churches too have seen similar teaching, encouraging 'holiness' if not 'perfectionism.' Wesley's hymn 'Love Divine' expresses this: '…take away the love of sinning…'

The clearest biblical inspiration of this idea is found in 1 John. 'No one who is born of God commits sin…' (3.4–9 also 5.19). This poses problems! It does not tally with the experience of most Christians, including great saints, and it contradicts John's own words. 'If we say we have not sinned…we make [God] a liar' (1.8, 10). Either John thinks most of his fellow believers are not born of God, is confused, or we misinterpret him.

Judith Lieu (1991, p 59ff) reminds us of the eschatological milieu. When the end-time came, the sons of light would be free from sin (T Levi 19.9 and 1QS4.21f). For Johannine Christians that time had come in Christ's resurrection. Caught up with him in the new age, Christians must share his freedom from Sin, if not from actual occasional sins. This distinction between *sin* as a power in the world, and *sins committed* may explain how John's heretics got their ideas, but it cannot be sustained throughout the letter to explain *his* teaching.

Actions, not states of being, count for John

Alternatively, believers 'cannot sin' because they will not be part of *the* apocalyptic *Sin* of rebellion against God. But John is not using sin narrowly, to mean rebellion, unbelief or schism. He does not elaborate on 'the works of the flesh,' but sin has moral connotations. 'The Son of God came to take away the *deeds* of the devil' (3.8). These deeds include impurity and neglect of love.

Actions, not states of being, count for John. His readers *are* children of God but he does not read their future sinless glory back into the present. 'He who does right is righteous…' Nor is this the Pauline idea of imputed righteousness. Jesus will cleanse from all unrighteousness, but John still expects Christians to avoid sinning now (1.9; 2.1, 2).

So when John says Christians do not sin has he been carried away by his polemic situation? His opponents claim to be sinless; sin has no significance, or their status means that whatever they do is not sin, however immoral it seems to outsiders. John is scandalized. They are sinning; real Christians do not! Lieu concludes that freedom from sin is too central to John's thinking to be mere reaction to opponents. She undervalues this explanation. The letter *is* a response to conflict, and 3.4–9 are among its most confrontational verses, even if John might have said something similar in calmer times.

Lieu finally suggests that John was citing an existing text about right and wrong in the new age. It reassures his churches that they are in the right with God, while encouraging a truly moral lifestyle. Because it is not his own words (and may be pre-Christian) it fits imperfectly with his other points about sin. I believe it is too easy to resolve problems by postulating incompetent redaction.

So what alternatives do we have? Stephen Smalley (1984, pp 159–176) classes the explanations as grammatical, theological or situational. We have already seen the suggested distinction between 'Sin' and 'sins.' Another idea (favoured in the NIV translation, by Johnson [1993, p 69ff] and Stott [1964, p 135]) depends on precise use of tenses. Christians may commit one-off sins (an 'instantaneous' tense) but do not persist in sinning (the continuous present). This puts a deal of weight on grammar. Would John's readers be that precise? Possibly; a similar distinction exists in Aramaic. Though Smalley is not convinced, this remains attractive.

On this understanding, John describes a pattern of Christian experience in which sins may be committed but are out of character and will immediately prompt penitence, in the knowledge that forgiveness is available from Christ the propitiator. A Christian does not go on sinning.

This is not far from some theological explanations. The Wesleys prayed for the 'love of sinning' to be 'taken away,' and distinguished between high-handed and unconscious sins. Others cite John's own distinction between mortal and forgivable sin at the end of the letter—but why wait two chapters before clarifying this meaning? Or was Bede right in focusing on v 6, 'he who *abides* in him'? So long as we truly abide in Christ we will not sin. This too is attractive, but Smalley reminds us of v 9, '…he *cannot* sin.' So is this actually the solution? Should we read it '…he can *not-sin*'? 'The writer is describing a spiritual potential on the part of the believer.' (Smalley, 1984, p 161). Although he knows the present reality of sin, John picks up the inter-testamental idea that perfection is the gift of the Spirit in the Messianic age. I am not convinced. Greek requires different phrasing.

Smalley then, rightly, considers John's situation. This is not a calm discussion of morality. His opponents believe they are beyond the reach of sin; John responds that real actions define a state of grace. Either the polemics led him to exaggerate in ways which caused problems once the context was forgotten, or he quoted their slogans in verses 6 and 9, refuting them in verses 7, 8 and 10. His readers would recognize the unwritten inverted commas. This seems to me to make most sense, and is one of the few explanations which adequately covers the phrase 'he *cannot* sin.' If so, John did not teach perfectionism, and all who teach sinlessness from this letter are mistaken.

Or perhaps the conflict was less bitter. John corrects misunderstandings of his gospel (13.10; 15.3) about being 'clean all over,' or having authority to remit sin (20.22f). Sinlessness is an obligation but not his readers' present state. But why use simple indicatives? John uses a rhetorical device, hiding the imperative in the indicative like Joyce Grenfell, whose schoolma'am was forever telling George, 'We don't do that.' John sets out the ideal, but knows that his friends, just as much as the dissenters, need forgiveness.

In chapter 3 I suspect John quoted his opponents. In chapter 5.18 we have this hidden imperative. This explains John's 'sin not unto death.' People told that Christians do not sin need reassurance that if they do it is serious, but not the end of everything.

Commentaries and Conclusions 6

Houlden (1973) sees 1 John as an attempt to adapt ancient faith to new situations, stressing the unfinished yet hopeful nature of the moral struggle. 'John' is concerned with practice, and reduces grand ideas to immediate practicalities. He ignores contemporary codes (for example *haustafeln*) since mutual love sums up his expectations and expresses a theological conviction about the community's life.

Johnson (1993) likewise identifies mutual love as key in John's ethics. His opponents' sin is failure to obey that demand. Concern with schism skews the range of John's moral discussion.

Smalley (1984, p xxvi) claims our author refutes ethical errors; Jewish members of the church treat the love command legalistically; Hellenistic members limit it to those whose views they share; John stresses love which is universal, and combines imperatives with the incentive 'he first loved us.'

Dodd (1946) drew attention to 1 John's echoes of the teaching about Christian conduct common to the early church.

For *Stott* (1964), John responds to his opponents' errors in what he says about ethics. God's self-revelation is ethical—to claim fellowship with him without appropriate morals is a lie. Christ came to do away with sin; lovelessness is at variance with that purpose. Mutual love is at the core of apostolic teaching. John used moral and social tests in his teaching on assurance.

Thompson (1992) comments that although these letters are about spirituality and conduct most attempts to set them in context focus on Christology. She sees catechetical material in 1 John 2.1, 7, 8, 15–27; 4.4–6; 5.18–20. God's character is described in moral terms. Salvation is a communal experience, not an internal state. John is encouraging the hesitant Christian, so those whom he criticizes are secessionists, not inconsistent Christians. The letters should be read as a whole—'Everyone who loves is born of God' cannot be isolated from verses about belief in Christ and obedience to his commands. Though John's dualism accepts no neutral ground, he knows that Christians may not be walking totally in the light to which they have committed themselves. Thompson adds that *ideas* are light or dark, and urges caution in judging *people*.

Brown (1982) believes that John's opponents taught that morality was irrelevant to salvation, but were not actually libertines (p 54). For John 'orthopraxy' was an essential part of spirituality and orthodoxy. John's problem was that his opponents could claim justification from the Gospel of John, which had de-ethicized the gospel message (p 79f). Both John and his opponents taught a form of perfectionism; John saw continued forgiveness as part of this.

Lieu's study (1991) deals with theology and ethics. She wonders whether John's presentation—as a debate—gives the impression of schism when the reality was divergent opinion *within* the church (p 15). Assurance is a key theme. What determines a Christian's birth from God is moral action—loving and believing—not determinism. Abiding in God describes *both* moral identity of purpose *and* mystical union, since the moral life is union with the community and its tradition as much as with God. In contrast with John's gospel, sin is not unbelief, but unrighteous action requiring confession (public?) and forgiveness. In saying that those born of God do not sin John offers a benchmark by which the community may assess itself, rather than exploring perfectionism. John gives several motives for moral behaviour: 'his' (Jesus'? God's?) commands; identification with 'the light'; future judgment; imitation of Jesus or conformity with God's nature; devaluation of 'the world'; and conformity with Christian character, such that there is no conflict between works and faith/love. Like most New Testament writers he does not fully integrate them with each other. I note that this offers a mixture of deontology, consequentialism and a character-ethics tied to community rather than individualism.

Conclusion

John's letters provoke as much disagreement now as their author faced in life. Those with a conservative approach to biblical inspiration are naturally more inclined to take him on his own terms, offering assurance (itself a feature of conservative teaching) in a fraught context. Liberal critics recognize that context, but suggest that his response leads up a blind alley.

I find his ethics teasing. He says 'obey Christ's command to love,' but little about the content of that love. That itself exposes the nature of John's thinking. In outward form he stresses commands, but in practice his readers must exercise their conscience. They cannot rely on a casuistry which lists and so limits loving behaviour. John gives an example, refers them to Christ's character and mission, and says 'walk as he walked.' He tries to develop a supporting community which enables their choices, and within which (I believe) there is a repository of dominical teaching on which they can draw.

Faced with an ethical question, *'Who is my neighbour?'* Christ told a story and concluded with the question, *'What do you think?'* and the punch line, *'Go and do likewise.'* John sets the same challenge—to act, not merely discuss. In form he is deontological, but in practice his churches must respond, conscientiously and perhaps charismatically, to each situation appropriately in the light of Christ's love.

The Good Samaritan is an example of Jesus' ethical *method*, with which I believe John is consistent. John is accused of departing from the *content* of that story, at least as presented by Luke. (There is debate about Jesus' original point, see for example Linnemann, 1966, p 51ff). That *seems* true—John stresses love within a *narrow* community—but he is *developing* Christ's teaching and practice for his own new situation without denying the broader love-ethic. In the process he offers insights into the moral character of God and the moral essence of Christian communities.

John gives few specific answers to the question, *'What am I expected to do?'* but sets a greater challenge—*'Is your church enabled to answer that question for itself?'*

Bibliography

Atkinson, D J and Field, D H, *New Dictionary of Christian Ethics and Pastoral Theology* (Leicester: IVP, 1995). Especially see under 'Love' and 'Sin and Salvation'

Bauckham, R, 'James and Jesus' in Chilton, B and Neusner, J (eds), *The Brother of Jesus* (Louisville Kentucky: WJK, 2001) pp 100–136

Brown, R E, *The Epistles of John* (Garden City NY: Anchor Bible, 1982)

Dodd, C H, *The Johannine Epistles* (London: Moffatt N T Commentary, Hodder and Stoughton, 1946)

Edwards, Ruth B, *The Johannine Epistles* (Sheffield: Sheffield Academic Press NT Guides, 1996)

Fletcher, J, *Situation Ethics* (London: SCM, 1966)

Hart, C, *The Ethics of the Gospels* (Grove Ethics booklet, E 111)

Houlden, J L, *Ethics and the New Testament* (Edinburgh: T and T Clark, 1992)

Houlden, J L, *The Johannine Epistles* (London: Black's NT Commentaries, 1973)

Hays, Richard B, *The Moral Vision of the New Testament* (London: SCM, 1996)

Johnson, T F, *1, 2, and 3 John* (Peabody, Mass: NIBC, Hendrickson, 1993)

Liddell, H G, Scott, R, Jones, H S, McKenzie, R, *et al*, *A Greek-English Lexicon* (Oxford: OUP, 1940 edn) ('LSJ')

Lieu, Judith, *The Theology of the Johannine Epistles* (Cambridge: CUP NT Theology, 1991)

Linnemann, E, *Parables of Jesus: Introduction and Exposition* (London: SPCK, 1975) (hb 1966)

Manson, T W, *Ethics and the Gospel* (London: SCM, 1960)

Robinson, J A T, *The Priority of John* (London: SCM, 1985)

Sanders, Jack T, *Ethics in the New Testament* (London: SCM, 1986)

Schrage, W, *The Ethics of the New Testament* (Edinburgh: T and T Clark, 1988) (German text 1982)

Smalley, S S, *1, 2, 3 John* (Waco Texas: Word, 1984)

Stott, J R W, *The Epistles of John* (London: Tyndale NT Commentary, 1964).

Theissen, G, *Social Reality and the Early Christians* (Edinburgh: T and T Clark, 1993)

Thompson, M M, *1–3 John* (Downers Grove: IVP NTC, Ill, 1992)

Witherington, B, III, *The Jesus Quest* (Carlisle: Paternoster, 1995)